T0203187

APPLE THIEVES

Born in Saskatchewan, Canada, Beverley Bie Brahic grew up in Vancouver; today she lives in France. *Apple Thieves* is her fifth collection of poetry after *Catch and Release*, winner of the 2019 Wigtown Book Festival Alistair Reid Pamphlet Prize; *The Hotel Eden*; *The Hunting of the Boar*, a 2016 PBS Recommendation; *White Sheets*, a 2013 Forward Prize finalist for Best Collection and PBS Recommendation; and *Against Gravity*. Her many translations include books by Yves Bonnefoy, Hélène Cixous, and Charles Baudelaire; *The Little Auto*, her selection of Guillaume Apollinaire's First World War poems, was awarded the 2013 Scott Moncrieff Translation Prize; *Francis Ponge: Unfinished Ode to Mud*, was a finalist for the 2009 Popescu Translation Prize. She has received a Canada Council for the Arts Writing Grant and fellowships at Yaddo and MacDowell.

Also by Beverley Bie Brahic

Poetry
Against Gravity
White Sheets
Hunting the Boar
The Hotel Eden
Catch and Release

Poetry in Translation
Francis Ponge: Unfinished Ode to Mud
Guillaume Apollinaire: The Little Auto
Yves Bonnefoy: The Present Hour
Yves Bonnefoy: Rue Traversière
Yves Bonnefoy: The Anchor's Long Chain
Yves Bonnefoy: Ursa Major
Charles Baudelaire: Invitation to the Voyage

Apple Thieves

BEVERLEY BIE BRAHIC

CARCANET POETRY

First published in Great Britain in 2024 by
Carcanet
Alliance House, 30 Cross Street
Manchester, M 2 7 A Q
www.carcanet.co.uk

A CIP catalogue record for this book is
available from the British Library.

ISBN 978 1 80017 429 0

Book design by Andrew Latimer, Carcanet
Typesetting by LiteBook Prepress Services
Printed in Great Britain by SRP Ltd, Exeter, Devon

The publisher acknowledges financial
assistance from Arts Council England.

CONTENTS

i

ii

iii

for

Lucie, Sula, Cora and Isla

APPLE THIEVES

i

CAMOUFLAGE

Charles de Gaulle Airport
Paris, September 12, 2001

Rerouted mid-Atlantic
Behemoths like bison
Graze the tarmac. Soldiers
In combat dress
Stop cars stopping
Move on
       shrug their guns
As her small silhouette
Without baggage
Stumbles past accident tape
Into the pickup lane –
Returned unscathed
To the airport she departed from.

    *

Today again I am waiting
At the airport for a child
To return from a journey
One of the lucky ones
O ye gods of camouflage
Home to the suburbs
Where summer's fullness
Garnishes our table –
Market peaches, plums
From a tree the wind
Sowed in our yard –
Small acts of propitiation.

APPLE THIEVES

In his dishevelled garden my neighbour
Has fourteen varieties of apples,
Fourteen trees his wife put in as seedlings
Because, being sick, she wanted something
Different to do (different from being sick).

In winter she ordered catalogues, pored
Over subtleties of mouth-feel and touch:
Tart and *sweet* and *crisp; waxy, smooth*
And *rough*. Spring planted an orchard,
Spring projected summers

Of green and yellow-streaked, orange, red,
Rusty, round, worm-holed, lopsided;
Nothing supermarket flawless, nothing imperishable.
Gardens grow backwards and forwards
In the mind; in the driest season, flowers.

Of the original fourteen trees, five
Grow street-side, outside the fence.
To their branches my neighbour, a retired
Accountant, has clothes-pegged
Slips of paper, white pocket handkerchiefs

Embroidered with the words:
The apples are not ripe, please don't pick them.
Kids had an apple fight last week.
In September, when the apples ripen,
Passers-by are welcome to pick them, even

Those rare Black Diamonds that overflow
The wall. Sure, I may gather the windfalls.
Mostly it's squirrels that toss them down.
Squirrels are wasteful. Squirrels don't read
Messages a widower posts in trees.

MORE SQUIRRELS

Last night's Olympic skaters
Scored their figures in the ice
With mathematical precision
And unflinching grace.
Today, around the green oak
Whose branches shamble east
Quicksilver squirrels chase,
They twist and turn, sit back and feast,
They look to fall but never do.
Seated at my desk, I leaf
Through the oak tree for a word
To say exactly what I feel –
But really what I'm doing as they
Run circles round the oak
Is begrudging them their lightness –
And is it play, or is it work?

THE KUMASI BUS

When I was a girl – young woman rather – living in Ghana
I'd hop on my sky-blue scooter to shop in the village market,
But for Kumasi's, I flagged down a bus.
In palm-frond sun hats, round and vast as sun-umbrellas
Market women hawked juiciest
Gold-tipped pineapples, silken mangoes to weigh on the palm
                                                    of my hand,
Swathes of brightly-patterned cloth
Sized to make ravishing sundresses.

In my mind I am still that girl, bound for market with her Bolga
                                                    basket,
Gawking at cockatoo-yellow bananas
Shimmied through the crowd on the swaying head
Of a farmer with a singsong sales pitch:
Tastes, feel, colour, smell, voices husky or treble –
Rummaging in my basket I can still find it all,
Not a hint of a bruise.

Nowadays, however, I live in Paris, where for a night
                                or two
I bunk in hospital, in a room
Shared with a West African woman. 'Eight sisters,' she confides
After our surgeries, 'four born in Mali,
Four on the periphery
Of a Loire Valley town' – and one sister bustles in –
Now their talk and laughter start to swell our room –
Night dense with stars
A large, listening dark

That takes me back to the Kumasi bus –
SLOW AND SURE WINS THE RACE! – boasts the side of the bus
That will depart when it is full.
No one is looking at a watch.

HIGH LIFE
for and after Bernard O'Donoghue

Unlucky the girl who never leaves home
Who never savours the taste of exile
In a land where her pupils line up on Sunday
And each girl braids the hair
Of the girl in front of her
Until they come full circle and the last
Braids the hair of the first;

Unlucky the girl who never leaves home
To sleep under a tin roof vultures prance on
In a compound surrounded by coffee and cocoa beans
Where her pupils gather on washday
To launder patterned pieces of cloth
And spread them to dry in the lion sun
On scarlet hibiscus that perfume their dormitory;

Unlucky the girl who never leaves home
To live where the coast road becomes the road
                                    to the interior,
Close to a village whose wise physician
Proposes she come for a consultation
For she at twenty-two is childless
And seems to have chosen a sky-blue scooter
And foreign travel over the delights of a family.

MAHABHARATA
Peter Brook, Avignon-Paris 1985–2015

Tales within tales of dynasties,
Grief muted by battle cries,
And the trickle of their telling
Beyond history
Rise from the repurposed quarry
Night after Mediterranean night
Filmed for posterity.

Now, thirty years later in Paris
In the Bouffes du Nord Theatre,
Riches and poverty contend
On our retinas as the images
Dissolve, house lights dawn
And hands lift mismatched
Kitchen chairs onstage for the cast

Who will talk and take questions;
Old troupers, veterans
Jovial in t-shirts and jeans,
Krishna, Arjuna, Eternal Youth,
Their wizened avatars,
Terror and pity resolved
In the old vaudeville theatre

In Paris's immigrant quarter.
Economies of indigence
In which nothing endures
And nothing ends. Silence
In the house until a voice
From the gods calls down,
'Dharma,' it asks, 'What is dharma?'

WHEN THE CIRCUS CAME TO TOWN

They chained the elephant to a plot
Of grass beside the municipal pool.
I'd swum my lengths and towelled off
When I caught sight of her diffident bulk,
Rhubarb-leaf ears to capture breezes,
But shifting foot to foot uneasily
Like a visitor doubtful of welcome.
I caught her eye and she, I felt, held mine
As if we had something to say
If only we could find the words.

THE GYPSIES

There's a fire under the trees:
you can hear its low voice
speaking to the nation that sleeps
at the doors to the city.

If we walk in silence
– we brief souls –
among the dark domains,
it is for fear you should die,
perpetual murmur
of the hidden light.

after Philippe Jaccottet, *Les Gitanes*

ARRIVALS LEVEL
Just walk normal past the dog.

i

Was it wrong of me to ask
The immigration officer
Why we must do everything twice:
First the automated, then
The human-op machines?

> *I can't stamp your passport.*

Shuffling forward, papers in hand,
I'd speculated it was a test
Of automation before the human
Beings were declared redundant

> *It gives you two chances to lie to us.*
> *Follow me*

To Secondary Screening,
Holding pen for the dispossessed,
Granny, hair raked back
In a sari in a wheelchair;
A Mitteleuropean who
With all his anger on the surface
Frightens me –

> WHY AM I HERE?!
> HOW LONG IS IT GOING TO TAKE?!
> TWENTY MINUTES?! TWO HOURS?!
> WHY WON'T YOU TELL ME?!

Lord have mercy on us
We pray, heads down, in all our faiths.

Eastern Europe is manhandled
To another room. Sari grandma
Dozes off in a distant time zone
Where children bring her cool water
In cupped hands. Does she dream

     of how she gave away her cooking pots
     of how red the dust smelled after rain?

Now and then a petitioner is summoned
And handed his/her documents
As in an hour or two someone
Will hand me mine, saying, *'Welcome back...'*

Don't ask.
You saw what happened to Middle Europe.

ii

Girth of a punching bag
The duffel Viktor's stuffed
Between his knees. Lunch consumed
He cradles it like
Something ailing
Pivots to the small-paned door
With its decent curtain
Pausing to run his hands
His large useless hands
Under the cold tap;
Next he tugs on the door
And December barges in.

La porte! the other diners
Shout in French, Romanian
Polish, Russian… The
Spoons speak only hunger.

iii

So far we've been lucky
In our democracy.
Sure, every week we meet
A few budding tyrants
With their humiliations
Suffered and passed on.
But do we mouth *fuck you*
At Immigration, jobs
Office, the kiddies' school?
Anger can be costly.
Besides, how reprove
This person whose day broke
Over sirens wailing,
Snarled traffic, a child
Pestering for pennies?
Let's just hope they never
Inherit the earth.

NEWCOMERS

i

While his teacher spits and polishes
A few nuggets of English grammar
For the newcomers, Diego dreams
He vaults the window and saunters
Towards the Seine and villages
Whose gravel lanes and orchard walls
The 19th century painted
Over and over, determined
To record every nuance of the light.

In the satchel with the supplies
He packs for school each day – matches, tinder –
Diego has a cautionary tale
About a man who travels north
In search of gold, a man skilled
At things but not their reasons
Who with night falling, matches damp
And an unreadable dog,
Freezes to death, a mile from camp.

Autumn in a meander of the Seine
And a family from one of the Gulf States
Enrols their daughters
In infant school, and in the middle school,

A pair of sons. Mother
In the desert-coloured robes of her country
Looks on like the good fairy
Ready to bless the cradle; dad's all efficiency

In dark suit and tie. I'm that small
Background figure taking copies from a machine
That has no place in this tableau.
'Now then,' Mrs James is saying,

Embracing the little group
With her kindly smile,
'Now then, children, tell me,
What are your Christian names?'

*

One boy was in my English class.
I helped him with homework
And he drew pictures

To illustrate what home was like,
The men's side and the women's side.
For the New Year

He brought me a gift of dates,
And I pictured an oasis
Like one I entered long ago in Ghardaïa:

Water rilling through canals
Under proud palm trees
Like a prophecy of paradise

In which water stands for hospitality
And dates mean plenty.
But what I also remember

Is how, when I bent unthinkingly
To hug him in the bland school corridor,
His body recoiled.

CRÈCHE

Bonne Maman, your crèche this year has shrunk.
No bigger than my fingernail
The figures your Italian potter father formed
Gather in an abalone shell
We found in California. They could be
Grains of sand among the papier-mâché rocks.

The Wise Men have been delayed. Tomorrow,
Epiphany, you will lift them
From their shoebox bed and set them
With the villagers, their flocks and holy family –
Father, mother, child – safe for now
In their corrugated cardboard shed.

A DREAM CATCHER FOR KATE

I gave the child a dream-catcher
An orb of coloured yarns and beads
And fluffy pigeon feathers
Hooped to hang above her bed,

And in unsteady, rainbow-coloured
Letters on sky-blue paper, she wrote
Back, 'Thank you for my dream-catcher
I think it's working'.

ii

ROOT VEGETABLES

In 1912, the British Columbian, *a conservative local newspaper, recognized that Chinese farmers in Burnaby had turned "what was little better than a cranberry marsh into a richly productive area which is one of the most valuable assets to the municipality." –* N. R. Gibb, *Parallel Alternatives: Chinese-Canadian Farmers and the Metro Vancouver Local Food Movement.*

Remember how we lived on a street
Named for one of Britain's great men,
Where if pretty Mrs McTavish
Pulled her upstairs blinds after lunch
On a school day, phones
Would jingle? Remember the apple tree – cookers –
That cast a spell of shade, the cool
Dark cellar lit with jams and preserves?

Remember the garden shed
Where our doctor father stored the pizza
A proud papa from Italy
Baked and delivered hot from the oven
Like an 8-lb son?
We were a meat-and-potatoes household.

I remember Ho, market gardener,
Who once a week parked his truck on our street
While our mothers picked over
Baking potatoes, parsnips, carrots
Pulled fresh that morning from the earth's warm bed.

Did I think that Ho's name was 'Hoe'?
I read online that 'Ho' means 'together.'

Funny (funny strange) which stories
Sprout roots in our memories:
Did Ho's wife and all his pretty ones
Die from the bite of a Black Widow?
Was *famine* too abstract for the children we were?
Why this memory, not another one?

I remember how each December
Ho gave us a root
Dull and misshapen as a sweet potato.
Plant it, Ho said, in an earthenware pot,
Keep the soil warm and moist,
In the New Year it will bring you
Rich harvests and lots of babies.

Ho, this is for you and your mysterious roots
Still growing in a corner of my mind.
Things move into shadows and vanish;
Memory returns in an echo, as the poet Lu Chi said.

EXOSKELETON

The earth-mother forms
Of this chalky shell
Belong to a sea snail

Exoskeleton
Exhumed from debris
On childhood's tideline.

I can balance it
On the palm of my hand,
Trace the elegant

Mathematical spirals,
Slip into the
Voluptuous interior

Of this empty house
A nudge will set rocking
Almost indefinitely.

IN THE FIRST PLACE

i

Berries stipple the cliff, black, red
And green together on the canes;
Canada Geese patrol the shore,
Old wives with wicker baskets of laundry,
Quick to take offence – trespassers'
Footprints over freshly-mopped sand.

> *When I was down beside the sea*
> *A wooden spade they gave to me*
> *To dig the sandy shore*

Down from my acre of sunrise
With my pail for treasure, half-shell
To dig. The stairs steep, skunk
Cabbage beneath. Today they are blond
Fresh from a sawmill, bottom flight
Hitched like a fire escape. Private Property!

> *My holes were empty like a cup.*
> *In every hole the sea came up*
> *Till it could come no more.*

Once, through a hedge, I spied a home burial.
How did I know? I knew.
Wishing stones clanged in my pail,
Time sifted through my sandals.
Today I know memory is unfaithful
And the blackest berries taste best.

ii

Not forgotten, the house granddad built
Facing the mainland across Georgia Strait;
Like a long-house it was low to the ground
With tubs of fuchsia bells to ward
Off the primeval: unlogged, undivided,
Guarded by the plants grandmother favoured,
Old World species, gladiolus, sweet peas.
Granddad's fishing tackle hung in a crawl space
And when I visited he took me out
For a day of silence in a hired boat.

iii

We climbed the path to the railroad cutting
Where he left me to wait
While he slithered down
To ballast, sleepers sweating creosote,

Blood-draw and ripe berry smell,
Indian paintbrush, splotch of fireweed;
Unpocketed a good-luck coin
He laid on the rail, scrambled back up.

Together we watch the train bear down,
Headlamp sweep us
And recede to a dimensionless point
Always in the future, never free of fear.

The garden he kept along the tracks
Bore fruit summer long till autumn's
Green tomatoes, good for pickling.
What the child loves are the big suns

Facing west. They cut one or two
Packed with seed to carry back to the house
Above the beach, sea glass
And kelp, its amber holdfasts.

First, though, the coin of memory.
They peel it from the rail,
Thumb blankness
Where the face was. Smell creosote.

iv

The forest is a fragrant den, a web
Of dark desire paths
Descending towards the riverbed.

In spring and summer salmon leap,
Fall back and try again.
Would you call that *anxiety*? she wonders

As an angler
Plants his feet firmly mid-stream
To cast, reel in, repeat

Calligraphies of line written and effaced.
So what   she thinks
So what   the hit-and-miss   the splash

Iridescence you'll catch
Maybe, if you're lucky
Once or twice out the corner of an eye?

BLACKBERRY CLAFOUTIS

A recipe I downloaded
To my desktop
I keep thinking is a poem
Posted there

With its luscious title:
Blackberry irresistible surely,
Essence of
My north's high summer,

Its punitive guarded
Providence
When one morning
Is just imperceptibly

Cold enough to turn
The gas-burning
Pot-bellied stove on
For an hour

Before I let Anne's chickens out
And open the barn
Which smells sweet
Of hay bales, horses'

Bedding and berries
We picked along Blazing Tree Lane
Yesterday, arms, legs
And mouths bloodied.

We hid them in a freezer
Where they wouldn't rot
Before we make a clafoutis,
That French pudding

Cherry-studded traditionally
But cherries are ripe in spring
And we are headed for winter
Geese honking south, etc.

You should eat it hot
Directly from the oven,
Though it will still be good
For breakfast, tomorrow.

WORLD BOOK

Is it the object lessons:
The *World Book*'s umpteen volumes
She as quiz kid won
Devising a question

Deemed worth *Asking Andy*
Sidebar to the funnies
In the Sunday papers?
How do spiders spin their webs?

But when the box arrived
And her secret was disclosed
She was forbidden
To keep them on her private shelf.

It'll teach you a lesson

On the contest entry
She'd signed her kid brother's name.
Resentment? You bet.
But their domes and orbs still lure her

Like the sex of mushrooms
Into her wet forests,
And their hammocks beckon
From unkempt corners.

MYTHOLOGIES

Oh! it's draining poorly, this shower!
Bottom viscous, sea lettuce green.
Each time I enter, it's as if I've been
Translated to a goblin glen and stood
Half-naked on a mossy rock, a flood
Sloshing my shins, prelapsarian species
Of rush and fern glommed to my knees.
Oh! It's draining poorly, this shower!
I'll be up to here in brackish water –
No, don't look down! There reflected
Are embryonic stumps, a kelpie head
Leering up – or down? – I'm baffled –
Can this be me, this half-formed creature?
If only I could turn into a flower.

THE CARDIGAN

Some women save their sanity with needles
– Medbh McGuckian

Knitting occupies slow dusks
Once kids are settled
In frames of their own, two's dishes neatly stacked:

Cable-knit, girl-child pink, buttons pearly,
That sweater scratched,
Heaven help us it scratched my skin!

She'd have thrown it over a summer dress
In the prairie town
Where girls were 'girls' until they married

And there was no sex:
'We were innocents, complete innocents.'
In the fog of time past

Mother is sore, still sore, sore all over
How her mama lit into her
When she came home, three months' gone,

Husband enrolled in the annals of war:
And him a doctor! I thought you'd wait –
'Pissed,' my sister says,

'Granny was pissed.' I understand now
How granny would fear
For the distant war's the child-saddled widow.

The sweater? I bundled it into a drawer,
Moved it house to house
In its tissue paper shroud –

Now can I post it in the Box Return to Sender?

This doesn't owe me anything
She'd mutter
Bagging clothes for Autumn's Bazaar.

I bury my face in the fragrance
Of mothballs.
Stitches cast on, stitches dropped –

Still itching, yarn of memory?
At last
Have you earned your keep?

VANITY

Again, my eyes meet hers
In the treacherous glass.
'Don't need makeup,' she pouts
As I rummage a bag
For the leftover tubes
Of seductive names
Incognito, Scarlet Letter
Cunning pots of paint.
See, I cajole, how *Fauve*
Enhances your gaze,
How a glint of *Twilight*
Deepens your mystery?
You steal a look in the
Utilitarian
Glass, and recall again
The smoky evening
A man – 'younger man'
You emend for the sake
Of precision –
Tried to pick you up
In the gilded lift cage
Of a foreign hotel:
Istanbul? *At my age!*

JIMMY

It was Jimmy who hung the cheesecloth sac
Of crimson marbles – shooters – from our tree
That night in April
So we'd rub our eyes at breakfast
Wanting to believe the sapling – earth raw
Around its feet – had fruited while we slept.

But when Jimmy swung out that morning –
Glitzy chrome and whitewalls sparkling –
Into oncoming traffic
Because the black van ahead was dawdling,
It was his brother Tom, riding shotgun,
Who cried: 'Jimmy! That's mother's coffin.'

MISSING THE BOAT

In the dream I'm late for the boat.
You know the one. With a railroad station
Airport concourse, a flight gate closed,
A ferry slip with bladderwrack fingers
To palpate the world, saying *Is this not me?*
Thinking *Love is difficult.*
From the oak tree starlings squabble;
Little cat paw, little snub-nose
Pressed to double glass, little moonface
Looking out, asking *Is this not me...?*
The ferry waits, no, the ferry departs.
Your body flickers like a lost earring.

INLAND PASSAGE

We stand above the beach
Watching the tall white ships
Sail north towards Alaska.
The eaves dispense shade with an even hand.

Woman who fancied a house
Where everything kept its place,
And a garden planted
With butter beans and apple trees,

Put away the hose, the trowel,
Scrub the dirt from your nails,
Let's sip a Scotch on the porch
While our supper bakes.

Memories – they're like one of those
Roly-poly toy clowns
You thwack and you thwack
But they won't stay down.

IMITATION

Far from your branch,
Little leaf so frail,
Where are you off to? – From the beech
Tree that bore me the wind has divided me.
Now turning it spins me
From the wood to the plain,
From the valley to the hill.
Where the wind goes I go,
Is all that I know.
I go where all things go,
The place where naturally
The leaf of the laurel goes
And the leaf of the rose.

after Giacomo Leopardi, *Imitazione*

CALIFORNIA: SABBATICAL

And here we are. No plans to stay.
It just happened the way stuff does:
If x then y . . . next thing we know
We're here until the end of May.

Eight years in May? 'Get a mortgage,' they say,
'A mattress from the big-box store,
Sleep like students, on the floor.
Never mind how many months of May.'

Home is over there with the albums,
Mittens, umbrellas. We bring the wedding
Teapot back, a dozen volumes
Of loved authors to dress bare shelves;

Two years, we thought we'd be away.
I miss the clouds, their silver linings,
I miss the pissed-on stones of history,
Bells meting out rich hours of everyday;

But here we are beside this fogbound bay,
Dry creek-bed whose crickets praise the stars,
Unless those blinking lights are aircraft
Circling. We're here until the month of May.

PARADISE

A legend persists that the town was named because it was the home of the Pair o' Dice Saloon – Wikipedia

The rain that's falling hard and fast
Looks as though it means to last
   Right through another day and night
Like epic downfalls of the past.

We're fortunate our ark is tight
Allowing for the odd termite,
   And our windows' double glass
Should keep our cabin warm and bright.

We pray this rain will help to douse
Wild fires that burn in Paradise (CA),
   Conflagrations that near and far
Imperil home in other ways.

We humans in our shelters are
Susceptible to flood and fire,
   As apt to perish in our lairs
As ants and honey bees and bears –

 Echo (faint)
As ants and honey bees and bears.
As ants and honey bees and bears

TALL TALES
for Nielsen and Carol Ann Rogers

Remember the kids' pet bunny you crushed
Walking a mattress down the stairs
And being a big man squashed it flat,
That fist-sized ball of fluff you'd warmed
In your pocket nonstop from Miami.

Now we have the one about the day
Your heart stopped beating. You were pecking
Your computer, Carol Ann beside you
Reading emails, 'I feel dizzy,' you said,
And laid yourself out on the threadbare Persian rug.

Carol Ann's heart stopped beating too, but first
She called Emergency, performed CPR
Till the paramedics, red lights flashing,
Tromped upstairs to resurrect you.
Sadly, you had to stop driving for Uber

Which you quite enjoyed: cash flow nil
But brilliant for your fund of tales
Like the one about the no-show you collected,
Drove to destination, rang up,
Thanked digitally, and gave a five-star rating.

WOOLGATHERING

In March when clocks trip ahead
An hour, a patch of yellow sun
Warms our condo deck after breakfast
And by degrees shifts from left to right.

This morning I put a deck chair
In its path, an empty flower pot
Upended for a footstool, laptop, book,
And mug of Instant steaming

Like the teacup in that Chardin,
The woman woolgathering at a table
Whose drawer stands open a crack
You want to close, or better, open wide

And see what's hidden underneath
The bar of shadow, brownish-red
Like the teapot (spout steaming) –
And all of this so solid but the steam.

My neighbour's deck in shadow still,
A man I hardly know
Who keeps a shallow, blue-glazed bowl
Filled with water for the birds.

The blue jay is back.
I watch her rummage through dry vegetation.
Same jay as last year?
Such permanence would reassure me.

Yesterday, on my way out to the shops,
He was seated with his eyes closed
In the chair I leave at our front door
Because in winter that's where the sun is.

Were you coming out to read here?
He asked. He knows my habits
I'm a little startled to discover.
Don't move, I say, I'm off to fill the fridge.

We're just tenants, after all.
'The sun feels good,'
He adds, shyly, 'I'm just enjoying
The feel of it on my skin.'

iii

MESSAGES FROM THE VAUCLUSE
for and after Pierre Brahic

1 August

The heat this week is breaking all the records
The village fountain drips tepid water.
Cycling? Only the English
Die at noon on the asphalt.
Three days camping in the Alps in search of a breeze,
Out and back without a breakdown.
Paul is going to purge himself
To improve the circulation of his blood.
Dogs hug the base of walls.

6 August

Thank you for your note
Which speaks of 'poem.'
Such an idea never crossed my mind
But here's a thought – poetry is
Where the reader finds it.
Of course, I leave my letter at your disposition
So you may give it a value
It doesn't in my eyes possess.
The interest of writing is to give what one doesn't have
To the person who least expects it.
So the critic makes his honey
And the author looks at himself in the morning
In order to love himself at night.
Only the woodcutter knows the grain of his wood.

8 September

The fig trees are producing figs
And the jam follows suit.

Catherine was here with her friends,
She removed the net
From under the mulberry tree
And now mulberries drop thick and fast into the gravel.
With your permission, I'll replace it.

The hunting season opens Saturday.
Paul will be there:
'I've only ever missed *l'Ouverture* once
For my military service in Tunisia.
      I still love dates.'

More and more wolves on the Mont Ventoux.
From the edge of the wood a boar
Eyes a cyclist
Who pedals towards the mountain's top.

Three red leaves on the grape vine.
The wood is cut.

WHY?

A remnant of blood orange moon
Smiles over the Dentelles at dusk:
Mona Lisa
Musing over the cryptic world,
And so much breath in this old mill house
Morning blurs the line of hills,
Roundnesses of belly and thigh.

We waken to the song of you
Trying new words in old questions:
Why a great grandma's manger scene,
Chipped shepherds and tinfoil stream?
Why the bunch of olive branches
Last winter's olives still adorn?
Welcome to the Age of Questions.

NIGHT SONG OF A WANDERING SHEPHERD IN ASIA

What are you doing, moon, in the sky? Tell me, what are you doing,
Silent moon?
You rise at dusk and set off
Contemplating deserts; then you rest.
Aren't you tired
Of the same old routes?
Aren't you bored, can you dream
Still of those valleys?
The life of a shepherd
Is just like your life.
Up with the first white light of dawn
He moves his flock across the plains,
Sees more flocks, more water, more grass;
When evening comes, worn out, he rests:
And this is all he expects.
Tell me, O moon: what good, to him,
Is a shepherd's life? What good to you is your life?
Tell me, where do they lead
My own brief wanderings,
Your immortal travelling?

***

Perhaps you understand this life on earth,
What our pains and sighs are;
What death, that ghastly pallor
Of our appearance is,
And what it is to pass from the earth
And the company of those we love.
And surely you understand

Why things are as they are, you see the fruit
Of morning, and of evening,
Of the infinite, mute, ongoing-ness of time.
You surely must know the love
That makes springtime laugh,
Whom heat pleases, and what winter
With its ice is good for.
You know and discover a thousand things
Hidden from a simple shepherd.
Often when I look at you so calm
Up there on the empty plain,
You whose circles touch the edge of the sky;
Or when, with my animals,
Step by step you follow me;
And when I look at the stars burning in the sky,
I ask myself:
But why all these flames?
Why the infinite space, the fathomless
Blue depth of sky? What does it mean,
The vast solitude? And what am I?

from Giacomo Leopardi, *Canto Notturno di un*
Pastore Errante dell'Asia

CYCLING TO THE COL

I love the look in early spring
Of fields turned over –
Earth well-fucked, gleamy clods

The plough churns up, its rumpled bed.
Soil ready for the seed.
'*Les femmes*! Best let them scold,'

Knee-deep in artichokes,
An old man declares, 'later you make up.'
Deft as a midwife, he thrusts

His hand into leaves, sizing up
The budding hearts, *tasty morsel*
The ancients claimed.

I climb – what? 2 mph? – not fast
Along hedgerows of adolescent juniper,
Dog rose, a few red hips

Still arcing from the stems
Before the bloom, before new fruit is set
Fields prepare for spring.

NEXT TO NOTHING

Ambling back from the bottle dump
I wave to Sandrine, at work in the shade
Of honeysuckle's winter thatch.
'What weather!' we exult. 'Unseasonal,'
We amend, not to tempt fate.
Sandrine's stripping leaves from a sheaf
Of dried verbena to top up her tin
Of bedtime teas.
Verbena leaves that weigh next to nothing.

Beside the old cart track Paul's almond tree
Bursts into bloom – earth-light
To counter the unearthly moon
Phosphorescing this morning
When I stepped out with my armload of towels.
Almond blossom embalmed the air. . .
But what was that sound? Then the flash –
Honeybees, a swarm of them
Swimming in the almond tree flowers!

AT A LOSS

Madame Lafitte will be selling the house
She's called home since the day she wed.
Now it will go to her son and stepson.
She apologises for the kitchen
Which has not been redone, but she's proud
Of her cupboards, their depth
And capacity to keep things hidden.

We discover a structure, unfinished
Behind a shiny laurel hedge:
'Somewhere to put my husband's mother,'
Madame Lafitte the elder;
When he ran off, she stayed on with his wife,
And the cottage, what's left of it,
Has become a repository
For belongings we're at a loss
What to do with,
But cannot abandon – a pair of rush-seat
Kitchen chairs a new wife may be tempted
To mend, a dismantled bed . . .
You never know is our mantra.

No denying the view! In summer Madame Lafitte
(No longer the younger),
Likes to gaze late at the constellations
Of market towns down
On the Rhone Valley Plain – porch lights
We keep lit in the galaxy.

INFINITY

Ever dear to me, this lonely hill
And this hedge, which on all sides, almost,
Bars from view the last horizon.
But sitting and looking out, in my thoughts
I conjure up the unbounded spaces beyond,
And unearthly silences and deepest calm
Where but for little the heart is not afraid.
And as I hear the wind
Rustle among the leaves, I set
That infinite silence against this voice:
And I think of the eternal
And the dead seasons, and this present
Living season, and its sound. So, in this
Immensity my thoughts are drowned:
And to be drowned is sweet in such a sea.

after Giacomo Leopardi, *l'Infinito*

LIKE THE ANCIENT GREEKS WHO MEASURED THEIR WEALTH IN OLIVE TREES

i

From the road along his kitchen garden
I'm talking to Paul.
A pair of plane trees shade our two houses
With their common wall;
Cicadas drone *it's hot it's hot*
Till the sun sets and a breeze
Rises from Carpentras Plain . . .

In truth it is February, the year 2020
And a twinge of foreboding
Gains ground as surely as a pack of cyclists
Ascending the Mont Ventoux.
Paul rakes horse manure over his potato bed,
Tough work for a man of his age:
Ninety in October. Last October.

Daybreak – I listen for his door to bang
All's well with the world, I go back to sleep;
And again, at night
After he searches the face of the moon,
Its auguries:
A moon to plant and a moon to harvest,
A moon to prune, one to trim your nails.

One plot of spinach left and escarole
Whose outer leaves he tosses the hen –
Pene says she can count 35 shades of green

in my garden
Vine-leaf, artichoke, thyme and verbena,
Spinach and the ivy crumbling my wall –
Keeping only the frilled white hearts
Shielded from the light of the sun
Like asparagus whose purple tips
Will soon be poking up in market beds.

ii

Three months without cars on our road.
From his kitchen Paul watches
A starling couple spruce up last year's nest
In a low crook of the plane tree.
'They work hard,' he approves.
Same birds every year? I ask from the road –
We are keeping our distance now.
'Yes,' firmly – and who am I, Paul,
To question how you know?
Who planted our two plane trees?
You shrug:
Before your time, before your father's.

One field of cherry trees unsold,
And the olive trees you won't sell
No matter how much they'd give
To plant houses along that hill:
It's a crime to cut an olive tree,
And the rest, these quarantine days,
Comes from the village café-shop
Where on Sundays, religiously,
You pay what you owe. *On ne sait jamais.*

Tomorrow, I say, we'll go to Mazan
For asparagus. Straight white stalks
Not jetting to Paris-Tokyo-New York
These quarantine days.
Two kilos, you want, 'broken ones,
'I'll pay you.' 'I'll pay you,' you repeat.
Careful accounts
Make good neighbours: who first said that?

iii

Two days after our Covid shots,
Taking the step from garden to house,
You fall
And can't
Get up

You will bump yourself past vacant hutches
Down a flight
Of stairs to the kitchen, where you yank
The corkscrew-corded phone.
You're lucky, firemen scold, wrapping you
For the trip to town
In heat-retaining foil.

Neighbours scatter grain, 'a quarter
Scoop, no more!' and stale baguette
For the last hen, who pecks her eggs:
Elle est bonne à rien! The weeks
In rehab turn into months
And still you fulminate: Eat her!

Good for nothing! – Weren't those
Your mother's words for you?

Marou finds a home for the hen –
One chore less when you return.
On that day, when it comes,
Marou brings a store-bought chicken
Good for several meals,
Wrapped in heat-retaining foil.

CALM AFTER THE STORM

The storm has passed:
I hear birds rejoice, and the hen
Out chuckling
In the road again. There, looking west,
Above the mountain, is a patch of blue;
Fields and hills brighten,
In the valley, the river gleams.
Hearts are lighter; on all sides
The hum of folk
About their daily work resumes.
The artisan, job in hand,
Singing, appears in his doorway
To glance at the wet sky;
A woman hurries to draw water
Freshened by rain;
And up and down byways and lanes
The vegetable seller
Renews his cry.
The Sun is back, smiling on hills
And hamlets. Households open
Shutters, air terraces;
And in the distance, on the high road,
Bells jingle; the cart creaks:
The traveler's on his way again.

from Giacomo Leopardi, *La quiete dopo la tempesta*

ÎLE DE FRANCE

Northern skies, their opulent cloud,
New storms building on last night's ash;
New towns grafted to established ones
With a weekday market, granite church,
And a Monument to the Dead
Whose names survive in these parts.
You are 50 km from Paris–Notre-Dame,
We're crossing the in-between zone.

I write this in the illusory peace
Of an evening in the not-quite-real world
Of mega-hay rolls, warm manure piles,
Cabs of trucks unyoked from their loads
Frisking home, to mark our journey
Over back roads with time-hedged cottages
Whose shutters are still open,
Whose lamps are coming on.

THE ASSUMPTION OF THE VIRGIN

August 15th. We're a ghost town – just us
And the stand-offish widow,
Her jangly terrier and vintage Peugeot.

No sign of them street-side for ages now,
Although at bedtime
I can see her big screen flicker

And these sultry nights with windows
Open to whatever's out there
Watching with us, and most other houses

Silent as the grave, I hear the sound:
A treble call, the bass response,
One voice quavers, the other menaces;

I see my neighbour, ramrod straight,
Fingers knit in her lap,
Dog muted at her side. . .

A Western, by the frantic whinnying
And clatter of hooves,
In which Virtue talks back to Villainy,

From a position of weakness
It goes without saying; and the roses
Hold their sweet breath at the window.

STYLEBOOK

Spelled with a 'u'
Colour
Has more colour

Than *color*
Spelled without
A slight flavour

A *je-ne-sais-quoi*
Of the baroque
As misbehaviour

Might flatter
The neighbour
Holding the door

To the elevator
Cage on 2
A dapper silver-

Haired charmer
Who spells ardour
With a you.

THE UNMADE BED

I who delight in belongings
Handed-down, sun-dried linens
With asterisks of mending
Like footnotes to history,
Am ironing a sheet we discovered
In your mother's armoire,
Never slept on, or so it seemed,
Métis, a mix of linen and cotton,
Initials I read like Braille.

My usual lick-and-promise job,
Hands busy, head free to digress.
See? here's one of those reminders
I keep tucking into mirrors
Or posting on the fridge
Eye level with my shopping list:
Delacroix's *Unmade Bed*, sheets rumpled
As the morning after an orgy,
Rough seas at body temperature.

I dreamt we slept in such a bed,
Haggled with neighbours for one
Your mother, it transpired,
Then the new wife, gave them –
Good riddance, she thought.
Alas! cramped for post-romantics
It soon joined the chamber pots
In an attic splashed with sunlight
Through red tiles the mistral displaced.

There, I'm done ironing. What
Was she saving it for, I brood,
This wedding sheet I cherish
From my mother-in-law's trousseau?
Come help me fold it, will you,
Out here in the hallway
Where we iron out our tango steps:
Abrazo! Toe to toe, back up, stop,
Trying not to let our corners drop.

LITTLE SONG FOR MICHEL

Spread-eagled
Across the bed I lie
My mind blank
As a prairie sky

Till you come back
Showered shaved ready
For work
You pick your strawberry

Tie and the mirror's
Tremor catches my eye
It wants to dally
With you the way

A puff of wind
Will tickle the skin of a summer day
And one white cloud
May turn things hazy

AT MY WINDOW

Monday's shutters clatter wide
Upon the church's weathered face
Crumbling like a day-old baguette;
Pieces plummet,
Wake the drifter
Snug in the wall's rain shadow, dreaming –
Well, of what permanence
Must he in his broken shoes dream?
Scaffolding appears
Whose rungs midnight climbers ascend
Surreptitiously; whose metallic structure
Displaces our familiar vagrant,
A man faithful to his scrap of pavement,
Returning each day at nightfall
Home from his hunter-gathering.

Eight o'clock chime the bells of two churches,
Time for the tillers and toilers
To assemble their implements –
A pulley whose burden this fine morning
Is a freshly-quarried block of blonde stone:
Our old lady is getting a face-lift.

I think I'm beginning to understand
How our human monuments – temples,
Palaces – took so many lives to build.
Keeping this one upright is ruinous
Even with the odd movie deal.
What if we allow it to collapse,
Allow Mother Nature her way?
Imagine! City blocks of prime earth:

Room for climbing walls, caves
To hide and seek in, burnt-out trees
For our play houses.

From their summits midnight's climbers
Post images of terra-not-so-firma:
Gilded domes, a string of bridges
The river threads...

One pink-polluted dawn I watched
A pair of roof-climbers negotiate
The last toe-holds.
Soft as a cat the boy dropped,
Then the girl,
And they held each other for a long time
Before they rambled off into a sunrise
Smelling of piss and baking bread,
The city in its glory and dereliction
All ahead
Just as I was opening the shutters.

PEAPODS

April morning
Sun angled through a skylight
A small girl
Silken hair
Cut for the first time this week.
Yes, she concedes
On Facetime, my hair's been cut.

One toss of her head
And her bob starts to swing
Pendulum-like
Until it comes to rest
Against her cheek,
Proving what exactly?

Do I detect the ghost of a smile
As she tucks it
Like a comma
Behind her ear?
Coquette!

God of Lamarck
God of Mendel and his peapods
God of DNA and
Double helices

Tell me where oh where
Along the winding road
Of human history
With its tools and weapons
Did she acquire this charm
And was it
By chance or by design?

TANGO

Waiting for the porridge pot to boil
I practice Argentine tango
Extending first one leg, then the second;

And the silver kettle's gravid belly
Mirrors me in my blue nightgown:
My spine is straight, my arms curve round

As if to grasp a beach ball
Or that red balloon, the sun
Lifting from the puzzled rooftops.

One street over I see a girl
Leap to catch the string she never
Thought could get away from her so fast. . .

> *Mind what you're doing, or you'll fall!*
> *Move your right foot forward,*
> *Brush your left instep; flex*
> *Your knees the way Natasha said. . .*

Natasha Ng from Buenos Aires,
Who won't allow us to *Embrace*
Or dance C*ruzada* and *Boleo*
Until we learn to walk. *Caminar.*

Sun floods the room in the kettle:
Slotted spoon, plate of fruit, copper scales
To weigh and measure
From my husband's mother's Marseille pharmacy;

We could be a portrait, I think,
Portrait of a Woman in a Kettle.

MONARCH

Hey there, gorgeous
You with the flame-coloured wings
Dodging rush-hour traffic
Surfing the slipstreams

Just a fellow commuter here
Stuck in the Anthropocene
Waiting my turn to cross
Envious of your
wings

ACKNOWLEDGEMENTS

Warm thanks to the editors of the publications where a number of poems first appeared, sometimes in earlier versions: *The Fiddlehead, Literary Matters, London Magazine, The New Criterion, The Malahat Review, The New Yorker, Prairie Schooner, Poetry Ireland Review, Poetry Review, PN Review, The Robert Graves Review, Queens Quarterly, Southlight, Times Literary Supplement.*

Eleven poems were published in *Catch and Release*, which was awarded the 2019 Wigtown Alastair Reid Pamphlet Prize, and published in a design by Gerry Cambridge.

'Tango' was reprinted in *At Home: a collection of poems* published by Lautus Press, in 2023.

Christopher Reid has generously allowed me to borrow an image from his collection, *The Scattering*.

The lines in italics at the end of 'Root Vegetables' are from Lu Chi's *Wen Fu*, translated by Sam Hamill.